from SEA TO SHINING SEA

OREGON

By Dennis Brindell Fradin and Judith Bloom Fradin

CONSULTANTS

Thomas C. McClintock, Ph.D., Professor Emeritus of History, Oregon State University; Member, Oregon State Board of Education

Robert L. Hillerich, Ph.D., Professor Emeritus, Bowling Green State University; Consultant, Pinellas County Schools, Florida

CHILDRENS PRESS®
CHICAGO

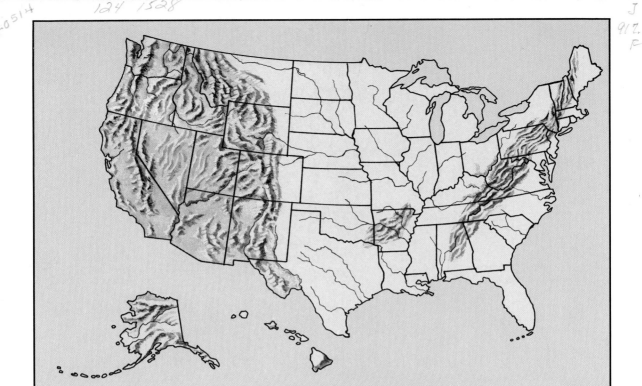

Oregon is one of the three states in the region called the Pacific Coast. The other Pacific Coast states are California and Washington.

For Sammy Ali, our friend and meticulous researcher

Front cover picture: Purple lupine and red paintbrush blooming near Mount Hood; page 1: Low tide at Cannon Beach; back cover, Proxy Falls, in central Oregon's Three Sisters Wilderness

Project Editor: Joan Downing
Design Director: Karen Kohn
Typesetting: Graphic Connections, Inc.
Engraving: Liberty Photoengraving

Library of Congress Cataloging-in-Publication Data

Fradin, Dennis B.
  Oregon / by Dennis Brindell Fradin & Judith Bloom
Fradin.
    p. cm. — (From sea to shining sea)
  Includes index
  ISBN 0-516-03837-0
  1. Oregon -- Juvenile literature. I. Fradin, Judith Bloom.
II. Title. III. Series: Fradin, Dennis B. From sea to shining sea.
F876.3.F69 1995
979.5--dc20   94-36725
                                               C   I   P
                                                   AC

Table of Contents

Windsocks flying during the Lincoln City Kite Festival

INTRODUCING THE BEAVER STATE

Oregon is a big state along the northwest Pacific Coast. Mountains, woods, and seacoast make Oregon a place of great beauty. That is why one of the state's nicknames is the "Wonder State." Huge numbers of beavers once lived in its rivers and streams. Another Oregon nickname is the "Beaver State."

Still another nickname is "End of the Trail." During the mid-1800s, thousands of pioneers traveled to Oregon. They followed the Oregon Trail, which was 2,000 miles long.

Today, Oregon leads the states at producing lumber. Oregon is also a top grower of potatoes and pears. Most of the country's grass seed is grown there, too. Pendleton woolens and Nike sportswear are goods made by Oregon-based companies.

The Beaver State boasts of much more. Where was children's author Beverly Cleary born? Where are the country's deepest lake and deepest canyon? Where do the Portland Trail Blazers play basketball? The answer to these questions is: Oregon!

Overleaf: A view of Face Rock and other seastacks on Bandon Beach, along the southern Oregon coastline

A picture map of Oregon

DUNNINGTON

Seacoast, Mountains, Fields, and Forests

Seacoast, Mountains, Fields, and Forests

Oregon is one of the three Pacific Coast states. Washington and California are the other two. Both of those states border Oregon. Washington is to the north. California and Nevada are to the south. Idaho is Oregon's neighbor to the east. The Pacific Ocean is to the west.

Oregon covers 97,073 square miles of land. Rugged, snow-capped mountains rise over parts of the state. Mount Hood is in the Cascade Mountains. It is Oregon's highest point. Mount Hood's snowy peak stands 11,239 feet above sea level. Between the Cascade Mountains and the Coast Ranges lies the Willamette Valley. Vegetables and other crops grow well in its rich soil. Most Oregonians live there. Far to the east, fields of wheat wave over the Columbia Plateau. Sagebrush and rimrock cover much of the southeast.

Woods, Wildlife, and Water

Roughly one-half of Oregon is wooded. The Douglas fir is the state tree. Pines, birches, cedars,

Mount Hood reflecting in Trillium Lake

The Douglas fir provides more lumber than any other kind of North American tree.

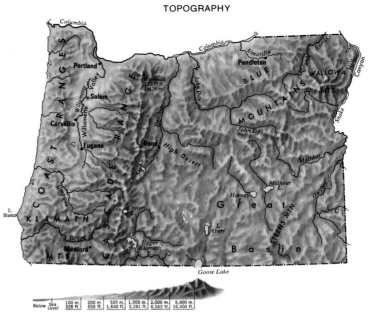

willows, and maples are other Oregon trees. The state flower is the Oregon grape. Other wildflowers are buttercups, Scotch broom, and Indian pipes.

Whales swim off the Oregon shore. Sea lions and harbor seals play along the coast. Salmon swim in Oregon streams. The salmon is the state fish. The beaver is the state animal. Beavers build dams on Oregon's lakes and streams. River otters fish along Oregon's rivers and streams. Bighorn sheep climb about the highlands. So do mountain goats. Pronghorn antelopes dash through eastern Oregon. The western meadowlark is the state bird. Long-billed curlews also nest in Oregon. Their beaks look like straws. Pelicans and puffins are two other Oregon shorebirds.

Left: A mountain goat with her kid

Sea lions (below) are seals that are larger than harbor seals.

9

The Columbia River flows for 1,243 miles through western Canada and the northwestern United States.

Water surrounds much of Oregon. To the west lies 295 miles of rugged Pacific seacoast. Two calm spots are Tillamook Bay and Coos Bay. The Columbia River forms most of the Oregon Washington border. The Snake River forms about half of Oregon's border with Idaho. The Willamette, Deschutes, John Day, and Malheur rivers flow within Oregon. The state has more than 6,000 lakes. Upper Klamath Lake is the largest. It covers nearly 150 square miles. Oregon's Crater Lake is 1,932 feet deep. That makes it the country's deepest lake.

CLIMATE

Crater Lake

The Pacific Ocean shapes the weather of western Oregon. Ocean breezes cool the land in the sum-

mer. They help warm it in the winter. That is why western Oregon has a generally mild climate. Along the coast, summer temperatures average about 60 degrees Fahrenheit. Winter days average about 45 degrees Fahrenheit. Ocean breezes also bring much rain and snow. Western Oregon receives between 50 and 130 inches of rain and snow each year.

The ocean breezes are dry by the time they cross Oregon's mountains. That is why eastern Oregon has hot summers and cold winters. Oregon's record high and low temperatures have been in the east. Parts of eastern Oregon receive only about 8 inches of rain yearly. Those places are deserts.

Yellow bee plants in bloom at John Day Fossil Beds National Monument

From Ancient Times Until Today

FROM ANCIENT TIMES UNTIL TODAY

Almost 200 million years ago, shallow seas covered Oregon. Sharks' teeth and crocodile fossils have been found in the state. About 50 million years ago, volcanoes began forming in Oregon. One volcano was Mount Mazama. It probably stood over 14,000 feet high. Volcanic explosions ripped away the mountaintop more than 7,000 years ago. Water filled the hole, forming Crater Lake. Mount Hood, too, was once an active volcano. It last erupted in the early 1800s.

AMERICAN INDIANS

The first people reached Oregon about 15,000 years ago. Many of those early people lived in caves. They left stone weapons and burial mounds throughout the state. Their paintings and carvings on canyon walls and cliffs can still be seen.

By the 1500s, many present-day Indian groups lived in Oregon. They included the Chinook, Nez Percé, Bannock, Modoc, Klamath, and Cayuse. In western Oregon, the Indians built houses of cedar

Opposite: In 1993, to celebrate the 150th birthday of the Oregon Trail, a wagon train traveled the path of the pioneers from Missouri to Oregon City.

These ancient rock carvings in the Columbia River Gorge National Scenic Area depict a thunderbird and an owl.

logs. They hunted deer and elk with bows and arrows. The western Indians traveled by canoe. They fished for salmon with grass nets.

Life was harder in dry eastern Oregon. Indians there built wickiups. These huts were made of branches and grass. They fashioned sandals and skirts from sagebrush and bark. To keep warm in winter, they made rabbit-skin robes. They gathered pine nuts, birds' eggs, and grasshoppers for food.

EUROPEAN AND AMERICAN EXPLORERS

Bartolomé Ferrelo, a Spanish explorer, sailed along Oregon's coast in 1543. Francis Drake, an English explorer, reached Oregon's coast in 1579. Captain James Cook, another Englishman, arrived at Yaquina Bay in 1778. These explorers sought a waterway between the Pacific and Atlantic oceans.

In 1792, Robert Gray, an American sea captain, came to Oregon. It was his second voyage to the Pacific Northwest. He discovered the mouth of the Columbia River. Gray sailed his ship *Columbia* several miles up the river. Along the way, he traded with the Indians.

In 1804, Meriwether Lewis and William Clark headed northwest from Missouri. They traveled

Captain Gray named the Columbia River after his ship. Until that time, the river had been called the Ouragon or the Oregon.

overland to find the Pacific Ocean. These explorers reached Oregon's Pacific Coast in November 1805. Near what is now Astoria, they built Fort Clatsop. They wintered there before returning east. Lewis and Clark then reported that Oregon was rich in fur-bearing animals. From Gray's and Lewis and Clark's travels, the United States claimed Oregon. Oregon included all the land between the Rocky Mountains, California, and Alaska.

A replica of Fort Clatsop, near Astoria

FUR TRADERS AND SETTLERS

In the early 1800s, American, English, and French fur traders came to Oregon. They exchanged goods with the Indians. Beads and mirrors were traded for beaver, deer, and sea-otter skins. These were used to make clothing.

In 1811, John Jacob Astor's Pacific Fur Company came to Oregon. That American company built a trading post in Oregon. It was named Astoria in honor of Astor. Astoria was Oregon's first non-Indian settlement. It was also the first American settlement west of the Rocky Mountains. Today, Astoria is Oregon's oldest town.

In 1812, the United States and England went to war. During the War of 1812 (1812-1815), Americans feared that England would seize Astoria.

Left: Oregon Trail pioneers carved these names on a canyon wall near Green River Crossing. Right: An Oregon Trail diorama at the National Historic Oregon Trail Interpretive Center near Baker City

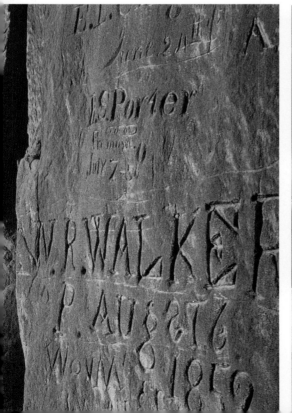

So in 1813, they sold Astoria to the North West Company. This was an English fur-trading company in Canada. In 1821, the North West Company became the Hudson's Bay Company.

John Jacob Astor

Canadian-born John McLoughlin ran the Hudson's Bay Company in Oregon (1824-1846). He kept peace with the Indians. He set up sawmills. On the north side of the Columbia River, he built Fort Vancouver. McLoughlin also allowed American settlers to live south of the river. McLoughlin is remembered as the "Father of Oregon."

In the early 1840s, the Oregon Trail opened. It stretched from Missouri to Oregon City. The 2,000-mile trip to Oregon took about four months by wagon. Most of the pioneers settled in western Oregon's Willamette Valley. They built farms and towns. Salem was founded in 1840. McLoughlin started Oregon City in 1842. Portland and Corvallis were founded in 1845.

John McLoughlin (below) had long white hair. The Indians called him the "White-Headed Eagle." Eventually, McLoughlin became an American citizen.

England and the United States had both claimed Oregon for many years. In 1846, the two countries divided the Oregon land. Present-day Oregon, Washington, and Idaho became part of the United States. The land north of Washington belonged to England. The United States Congress made Oregon a territory in 1848. The Oregon

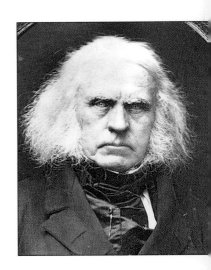

Territory also included part of Montana and Wyoming.

STATEHOOD, INDIAN WARS, AND INDUSTRIES

There are 640 acres in a square mile.

Congress passed the Oregon Donation Land Act in 1850. It offered men 320 acres of free Oregon land. Each man's wife could have another 320 acres. In that way, a couple could own 1 square mile of land. By 1850, Oregon had more than 12,000 people. There were four times that many by 1859.

Oregon's flag and seal have thirty-three stars because Oregon was the country's thirty-third state.

On February 14, 1859, Oregon became the thirty-third state in the Union. Salem was the new state's capital. Oregon's constitution did not allow slavery in the state.

Two years later, the Civil War (1861-1865) broke out. Eleven southern states had left the Union. They wanted the right to continue holding slaves. Many Oregonians sided with the Union. Most Civil War battles took place east of the Mississippi River. So Oregonians did not fight in that war. Instead, about 2,000 Oregonians fought to protect their land from the Indians.

Settlers had taken Indian lands. Few fur-bearing animals were left for Indians to hunt. Missionaries had taught Christianity to the Indians. They also tried to teach them that the Indian religions were wrong. Starting in the 1850s, the Indians began to fight back. The Rogue River War (1851-1856) took place in southwest Oregon. Gold miners there had polluted the Rogue Indians' fishing streams. When the war ended, the Indians were moved to an Oregon reservation.

Gold was also found on Nez Percé land in the 1860s. Soldiers forced the Nez Percé off their eastern Oregon land. In 1877, the United States government ordered the Nez Percé to move. They were to live on a reservation in Idaho. Under their leaders, one of whom was Chief Joseph, several groups

Survivors of the Rogue River War

Jeff Blevins

The Sunken Gardens at the 1905 Lewis and Clark Exposition in Portland

of Nez Percé fought back. But after many months, they surrendered. The Nez Percé were then sent to the Idaho reservation. By 1880, all of Oregon's Indians were living on reservations.

During those same years, more people poured into Oregon. They farmed and worked in its booming industries. Wheat farms and cattle ranches sprang up in eastern Oregon. Salmon canning became important. So did logging. Lumberjacks went into Oregon's woods. They chopped down pines and Douglas firs. Sawmills turned the logs into lumber.

In 1905, Portland hosted the Lewis and Clark Exposition. It honored the explorers' trip of 100 years earlier. About 3 million people visited Portland in 1905.

POLITICS, WARS, AND THE GREAT DEPRESSION

Oregon has been a leader in opening government to more citizens. In 1906, Oregon was the first state to hold an election for a United States senator. Oregonians elected Jonathan Bourne. But Oregon's lawmakers had to okay the people's choice in 1907. Until 1913, state lawmakers chose United States senators.

In 1912, Oregon become the sixth state to allow women to vote. Abigail Scott Duniway had led the fight for Oregon women. She lived in Portland and published a newspaper called the *New Northwest*. It was a voice for women's voting rights. In 1920, the Nineteenth Amendment to the Constitution was passed. It granted the vote to women in every state.

In 1913, Oregon was the first state to pass a good minimum-wage law. Edwin O'Hara, a

Abigail Scott Duniway (seated) signing the suffrage proclamation

Catholic priest, was the driving force behind it. The law assured workers a wage that they could live on. Millions of Americans worked long hours for low pay at that time.

In 1917, the United States entered World War I (1914-1918). Nearly 44,000 Oregon men served in the armed forces. Oregon's farmers and shipbuilders also helped win the war.

Eleven years later, the Great Depression (1929-1939) hit the United States. The whole country had hard times. Many Oregonians lost their jobs and farms. However, the United States government hired many jobless people. They built roads and dams. Many Oregonians helped build Bonneville Dam on the Columbia River. The dam was finished in 1937. Oregon's lumber business continued to do well. In 1938, Oregon passed Washington as the country's top lumber producer.

On December 7, 1941, Japan bombed Pearl Harbor. The next day, the United States entered World War II (1939-1945). The United States government feared that Japanese Americans might secretly help Japan. In fact, that didn't happen. Japanese Americans were among the best American soldiers. Yet, the government rounded up over 100,000 Japanese Americans. That included 4,000

Bonneville Dam was built during the Great Depression.

from Oregon. They were imprisoned in special camps. During the war, about 150,000 Oregon men and women served in uniform. Oregon-made cargo ships carried supplies to the troops.

New Growth and Changes

Americans flocked to the West Coast after the war ended. By 1960, Oregon's population was nearly 1.8 million. More people brought big problems. By 1961, factories had polluted the Willamette River. Fish could no longer live in it.

These five brothers were among the Japanese American residents of Portland who were sent to special camps during World War II.

In 1966, Tom McCall was elected governor. He promised to clean up the environment. He served from 1967 to 1975. Governor McCall signed more than one hundred laws protecting Oregon's land and water. By 1969, salmon once again ran the Willamette. In 1971, Oregon passed the country's first "bottle bill." It outlawed pull-tab cans. It also outlawed nonreturnable beverage bottles. McCall also signed laws to protect Oregon's beaches.

By 1980, Oregon's population had jumped to over 2.6 million. More people also were picking Oregon as a vacation spot. During the 1980s, the logging and lumber businesses ran into problems. Fewer people were building homes. So the sale of lumber fell. In recent years, the United States government passed laws to protect timberlands. These laws have limited Oregon's logging. Between 1982 and 1992, about 40,000 Oregon lumber workers lost their jobs. During those same years, other kinds of businesses have started in Oregon. They include electronic and computer companies.

The year 1993 marked the 150th birthday of the Oregon Trail. To celebrate, a wagon train traveled from Missouri to Oregon City. It followed the 2,000-mile path of the pioneers. Oregon hosted plays, rodeos, and festivals to honor the trail.

But Oregon is blazing a trail to the future, too. The state has pioneered two new programs. One is for health care. The Oregon plan will provide medical care to 450,000 uninsured people. Many of them are poor. The other program is The Oregon Educational Act for the 21st Century. Under it, tenth graders must pass basic skills and knowledge tests. Then they can choose college-preparation or job-training classes. By the year 2010, Oregon's school year will have 220 days. Oregonians want their children to be ready for the twenty-first century.

Recent laws to protect timberlands (right) have limited Oregon's logging businesses (left).

Overleaf: A boy feeding squirrels at Samuel H. Boardman State Park

25

Oregonians and Their Work

OREGONIANS AND THEIR WORK

Oregon has nearly 3 million people. Twenty-eight states have more people than Oregon. About 2.6 million Oregonians are white. More than one-half of them have German, English, or Irish backgrounds. About 115,000 Hispanics live in Oregon. They are the state's largest minority. Most Spanish-speaking Oregonians have roots in Mexico.

Asians are Oregon's fastest-growing minority. Between 1980 and 1990, their number doubled to 70,000 people. Most Asian Oregonians have Chinese or Japanese backgrounds. Nearly 50,000 Oregonians are African Americans. Almost 40,000 American Indians live in Oregon. The Umatilla, Wasco, Paiute, and Klamath are the largest Indian groups.

About 70,000 Asians and nearly 40,000 American Indians live in Oregon.

OREGONIANS AT WORK

About 1.3 million Oregonians have jobs. Service work and selling goods are the most popular kinds of jobs. Each field employs about 300,000 Oregonians. Service workers include people in

Picking Oregon cherries

A forest research lab worker in Corvallis

health care and law. Oregon's tourist business employs people in motels and hotels. Salespeople work in Oregon's department stores and food stores.

The government employs over 200,000 Oregonians. They include teachers, firefighters, and state lawmakers. Other government workers have jobs in Oregon's state parks and national forests.

More than 200,000 Oregonians make goods. The Beaver State leads the country at producing lumber. That is the state's top product. Oregonians turn out 6.2 million board feet of lumber a year. That is enough to build 200,000 three-bedroom houses. Oregon wood goes into buildings around the world. It is also made into paper, furniture, and other items. Many Oregon trees become Christmas trees. Foods, including frozen potatoes and bread, are Oregon's second-leading product. Scientific instruments and computer software are also made in the state. Pendleton woolens are well-known throughout the country. Headquarters for Nike shoes and sportswear is in Beaverton.

About 75,000 Oregonians are farmers. Oregon leads the country at growing filberts, also called hazelnuts. The Beaver State is also number one at growing grass seeds. Flowers, berries, potatoes,

wheat, and hay are other important crops. The state's farmers also raise dairy and beef cattle, sheep, chickens, and hogs.

A few Oregonians make their livings by fishing or mining. Salmon and shrimp are the top catches. Crushed stone and gravel are Oregon's top mining products. Oregon is the only state that mines nickel. Oregon mines more pumice than any other state. Dentists clean teeth with this volcanic rock.

A winter cattle drive near Madras

Overleaf: A twilight view of Portland with Mount Hood in the background

A Tour of the Beaver State

A Tour of the Beaver State

Oregonians and visitors alike ski and hike through Oregon's mountains. They go swimming and boating in the rivers, lakes, and ocean. They find its cities and small towns charming.

Up the Oregon Coast

Gold Beach is a good starting point for an Oregon tour. This town is found where the Rogue River meets the Pacific Ocean. It once was a gold-mining town. Today, Gold Beach is great for fishing. Chinook salmon and cutthroat and steelhead trout are caught in the Rogue River.

Port Orford is north of Gold Beach. This town of about 1,000 people has two claims to fame. First, it is the westernmost town in the United States, not counting Alaska or Hawaii. Second, the country's largest Port Orford cedar stands nearby. The tree is 219 feet tall. Its trunk is 37.5 feet around. Humbug Mountain is also near Port Orford. Hikers climb this 1,756-foot-tall peak. Close by is Cape Blanco Lighthouse. It has been guiding ships since 1870.

Horseback riders at Gold Beach

Blanco *means white in Spanish. Seashell fossils make Cape Blanco's cliffs look chalky white.*

Bandon is north of Port Orford. Bandon calls itself the "Storm-Watching Capital of the World." Big storms from the ocean strike there. Bandon is also called the state's cranberry capital. Each year, the town hosts the Fall Cranberry Festival. The West Coast Game Park Safari is near Bandon. Visitors can pet baby animals. They include snow leopards and raccoons.

Sunset Bay State Park is north of Bandon. The bay is enclosed by sandstone cliffs. That makes it one of Oregon's calmest and warmest places to swim. Oregon Dunes National Recreation Area stretches for 50 miles to the north. Some of the

Oregon Dunes National Recreation Area

sand dunes are over 500 feet high. People hike through the dunes. Some people explore them in dune buggies. At the dunes' southern tip is Winchester Bay. Whales can be spied from a whale-watching platform there.

Farther north is Sea Lion Caves. Visitors can see hundreds of adult sea lions and their pups. Newport is north of Sea Lion Caves. People go deep-sea fishing from Newport. Visitors also enjoy the Oregon Coast Aquarium. They view sea otters and a sixty-pound octopus there. The Spouting Horn is north of Newport. This is a blowhole. Seawater shoots skyward through cracks in the area's rocky cliffs.

A view of Astoria, at the mouth of the Columbia River

Astoria is in Oregon's northwest corner. This is the state's oldest town. A replica of Fort Astoria can be seen there. Nearby, Lewis and Clark's Fort Clatsop has been rebuilt, too. Rangers there wear frontier clothing. They show what life was like in the early 1800s.

PORTLAND

In 1845, Asa Lovejoy and Francis Pettygrove founded Portland. It was named for Pettygrove's hometown of Portland, Maine. Today, Portland is Oregon's largest city. About 450,000 people live there. As its name says, Portland is a port city. It lies along the Columbia and Willamette rivers. It is less than 100 miles from the Pacific Ocean. Ships travel along these rivers between Portland and the ocean. The city's port handles 60 billion pounds of cargo a year. Only three of the country's Pacific ports are busier.

Portland is called the "City of Roses." Each June, the city hosts the Rose Festival. A big parade and a rose show are part of the fun. Portland's International Rose Test Gardens have more than 400 kinds of roses. The gardens were started in 1917.

The port of Portland on the Willamette River

One of the floats in Portland's Rose Festival Parade

A noontime concert in Portland's Pioneer Courthouse Square

Mills End Park

Pioneer Courthouse Square is in the heart of Portland. Each brick in this plaza was paid for with money from a Portlander. The square has a sculpture that forecasts Portland's weather. The sculpture sprays water if it's going to rain. Portlanders picnic at the square. Concerts are held there, too.

Portland has the largest wooded city park in the United States. Forest Park covers nearly 5,000 acres. Portland also has the world's smallest park. Mills End Park is just 2 feet across. It was begun in fun in 1948 as a home for leprechauns. They are the elves in old Irish stories.

Portland has the country's oldest symphony orchestra west of the Mississippi River. The Oregon Symphony was founded in 1896. The city also has the world's second-largest hammered-copper statue. The 36-foot-tall *Portlandia* statue is of a sea goddess.

The City of Roses has fine museums, too. The Oregon Historical Society has displays on the state's past. Northwest Indian artworks are on view at the Portland Art Museum. Children enjoy the Oregon Museum of Science and Industry. Its hands-on exhibits include computers and a space station. The World Forestry Center shows visitors what woodlands mean to people. The Trail Blazers play pro

The Statue of Liberty in New York is the world's only larger hammered-copper figure.

Left: The USS Blueback *submarine exhibit at the Oregon Museum of Science and Industry*
Right: Portland's Portlandia *statue*

basketball in Portland. Their name comes from the Oregon Trail that ended near Portland.

OREGON'S HISTORIC CITIES

Oregon City is at the southern tip of Portland. John McLoughlin founded the town in 1842. His mansion, John McLoughlin House, dates from 1846. It holds many of McLoughlin's belongings. The "Father of Oregon" lived there eleven years. Oregon City was at the end of the Oregon Trail. From 1849 to 1851, it was the capital of the Oregon Territory.

The capitol, in Salem

Gresham is east of Portland. It is called the "City of Music." Gresham hosts the summertime Mount Hood Festival of Jazz. Beaverton is west of Portland. It was named for the many beaver dams that were once there. Beaverton hosts the Festival of Flowers each June. Nearby Tigard holds its hot air balloon festival that same month.

Salem is southwest of Portland. It was founded in 1840 by Jason Lee. He was a missionary from New England. His home is open to visitors. Salem is now Oregon's third-largest city.

Salem is also the state capital. Oregon's lawmakers meet in the state capitol. The present capitol was completed in 1938. It is one of the most modern-looking of the fifty state capitols. A figure called the *Pioneer* stands atop the dome. Inside the capitol are four large murals. They show major events in Oregon's history. Salem is also home to Willamette University. It was founded in 1842. That makes Willamette the oldest college or university west of the Rocky Mountains.

Corvallis is southwest of Salem. Oregon State University is there. The school's Horner Museum has mammoth and whale bones. In 1846, Eugene Skinner settled south of Corvallis. The town that grew there was named for him. Eugene is now

The Pioneer *statue on top of the state capitol*

A mural in the state capitol House of Representatives

With 16,000 students, the University of Oregon is the state's largest school.

Oregon's second-largest city. About 112,000 people live there. The town is nicknamed "Tracktown USA." Many runners train there. The University of Oregon is known for its track and field teams. The university's Museum of Art is well known, too. Ivory carvings from China are among its treasures.

Cottage Grove is south of Eugene. It has six of Oregon's fifty covered bridges. Oregon has more covered bridges than any other western state.

Medford is south of Cottage Grove. It was begun as a railroad town in 1883. Today,

The University of Oregon Museum of Art

Medford is Oregon's sixth-largest city. It is in pear country. Each April, the town hosts the Pear Blossom Festival. Jacksonville is just west of Medford. The town boomed after gold was found there in 1851. Today, visitors enjoy seeing Jacksonville's homes from the 1850s. Not far from Jacksonville is the 40-mile Rogue River Hiking Trail.

Oregon Caves National Monument is southwest of Jacksonville. The caves have 3 miles of passages and rooms. The largest room is 240 feet long and 40 feet high. It is called the Ghost Room.

Historic buildings along Jacksonville's California Street

The Paradise Lost Room at Oregon Caves National Monument

CENTRAL OREGON

Klamath Falls is east of Oregon Caves. The town lies on Upper Klamath Lake. That is Oregon's largest lake. The Favell Museum is in Klamath Falls. It has the largest Indian arrowhead collection in the West.

North of Klamath Falls is Newberry Crater. Until 10,000 years ago, it was a volcano. In 1991, the crater was named Newberry National Volcanic Monument. Visitors can see volcanic rock called lava there. Two lakes are inside the crater.

A few miles north is Bend. The town was named for a bend in the Deschutes River. Bend is

Left: John Day Fossil Beds National Monument
Right: A view of Klamath Falls

Oregon's largest city east of the Cascade Mountains. Today, Bend has more than 20,000 people. The High Desert Museum is near Bend. It features the people, plants, and animals of Oregon's dry lands. Visitors learn how the Indians lived in this dry area. Porcupines, great horned owls, and river otters can be seen outside.

John Day Fossil Beds National Monument is northeast of Bend. Fossils of 55-million-year-old plants and animals have been found there. Saber-toothed tigers once roamed that land. A town called Fossil is near the monument. There, visitors can dig up and keep fossils of 32-million-year-old tree leaves.

The Dalles is to the northwest. It lies along the Columbia River. In the 1800s, French traders named the town. The Columbia River's canyon walls reminded them of French village streets. *Les dalles* means "flagstone" in French. Today, the town is known for its old brick storefronts. The Dalles Dam has helped make the town a port city.

The Dalles Dam

Highlights of Eastern Oregon

Oregon's wheat farms and beef-cattle ranches are in eastern Oregon. Pendleton is a center for the cattle

43

and wheat industries. This city hosts the Pendleton Round-Up each September. There is a big rodeo. Indian dancers also perform at this four-day event.

East of Pendleton is Hells Canyon. It is on the Oregon-Idaho border. Hells Canyon is the country's deepest canyon. It is 8,023 feet deep. The Snake River carved it. Only the best hikers can climb in and out of Hells Canyon.

Baker City is southwest of Hells Canyon. It sprang up in 1861 after gold was found there. The First National Bank in Baker City displays gold nuggets found nearby. The largest one weighs about six pounds. Some mining towns became ghost towns when the miners moved on. Greenhorn is southwest of Baker City. It once had more than 2,500 people. Today, Greenhorn is the state's smallest town. As of 1994, only three people lived there! Farther southwest is the town of John Day. The Kam Wah Chung Museum is there. It is in a restored trading post. Visitors learn about the Chinese who came looking for gold.

Nyssa is to the southeast. It is close to the Oregon-Idaho border. Nyssa is known as the "Thunder Egg Capital of Oregon." The thunder egg is the state rock. Thunder eggs range from less than 1 inch up to 4 feet across. Thunder eggs are made

Hells Canyon is the deepest gorge in North America.

44

into fine jewelry. They come from land that had volcanic eruptions. Many have turned up around Nyssa.

Malheur National Wildlife Refuge is southwest of Nyssa. It is a good place to end an Oregon trip. The refuge is located close to Harney and Malheur lakes. It is a watering and nesting place for birds. More than 250 kinds of birds have been spotted there. White pelicans and trumpeter swans are two of them.

Malheur National Wildlife Refuge

Oregon has twenty national wildlife refuges.

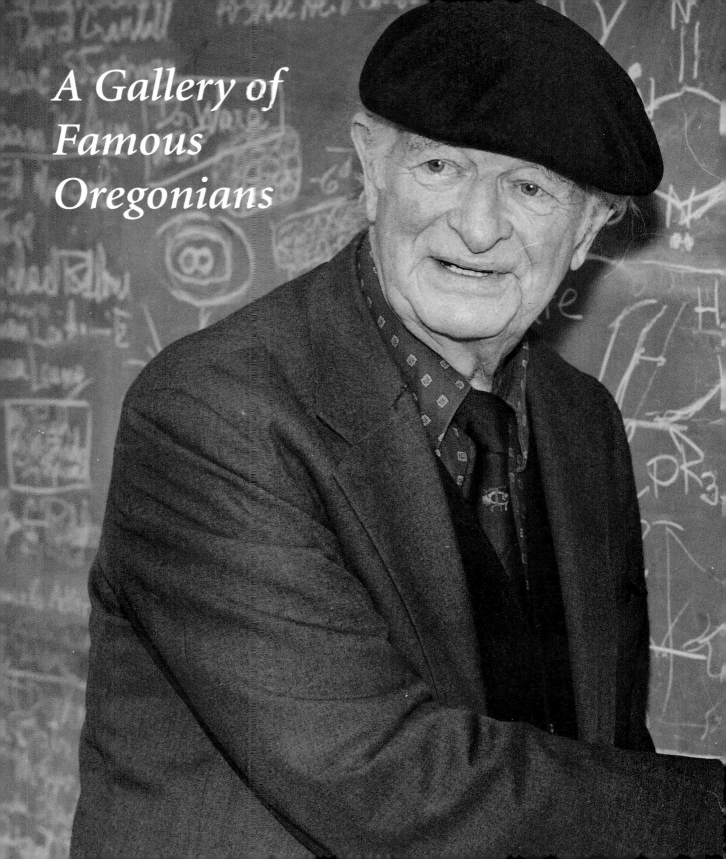

A Gallery of Famous Oregonians

A Gallery of Famous Oregonians

Oregonians have gained fame in many fields. They have become scientists, politicians, writers, and athletes.

Ing Hay (1862?-1952) was born in China. He came to the town of John Day in 1887. Many Chinese people worked in nearby gold mines. They came to "Doc" Hay when they were sick. He used herbal medicines to cure them. Today, his office is part of the Kam Wah Chung Museum in John Day.

Two men changed Oregon during the early 1900s. **William U'Ren** (1859-1949) was a political activist. He made it possible for Oregonians to elect their senators directly. **Oswald West** (1873-1960) became Oregon's governor in 1911. West reformed Oregon prisons. He set aside Oregon's coast for public beaches.

Scientist **Linus Pauling** (1901-1994) was born in Portland. He won a Nobel Prize for chemistry in 1954. It was for discovering how molecules work together. He also worked to stop the testing of nuclear weapons. For that, he won the 1962 Nobel Peace Prize. Pauling is the only winner of two different Nobel Prizes.

Opposite: Nobel Prize-winning chemist Linus Pauling

William U'Ren

Maurine Neuberger

Richard Neuberger

Mark Hatfield was born in Dallas, Oregon, in 1922. He taught at Willamette University (1951-1955). In 1959, Hatfield became one of Oregon's youngest governors. Seven years later, he was elected to the U.S. Senate. Hatfield spoke strongly against the Vietnam War. In 1988, he worked for the Wild and Scenic Rivers Bill. It protected forty American rivers. In 1995, Hatfield was in his fifth term as an Oregon senator.

Richard Neuberger (1912-1960) was born in Portland. His wife **Maurine Neuberger** was born in Cloverdale in 1907. Together, they served in the Oregon legislature. They were the first married couple to do that. In 1955, Richard was elected to the U.S. Senate. After he died, Maurine finished his term. She was then elected to her own six-year Senate term (1961-1967).

Portland was the birthplace of **John Reed** (1887-1920). Reed became a writer and reporter. In 1914, he covered the beginning of World War I in Europe. He also covered the Russian Revolution (1917). Back in the United States, he formed the American Communist Labor Party. The movie *Reds* is about Reed's life.

Yoncalla-born **Harold L. Davis** (1896-1960) wrote about frontier life. He won the 1936 Pulitzer

Prize in fiction for his novel *Honey in the Horn*. Davis also wrote *Distant Music*. Portland-born **Ernest Haycox** (1899-1950) worked as a trucker and logger. He became a writer of Western stories. His *Union Pacific* and *Stagecoach* became great Hollywood movies.

Phyllis McGinley (1905-1978) was born in Ontario, Oregon. By age six, she knew she would be a poet. McGinley wrote poems about family life. *Love Letters* is one of her books of poems. She also wrote *The Year Without a Santa Claus*. It is one of her many books for children. Poet **William Stafford** (1914-1993) taught at Portland's Lewis and Clark College. He also wrote more than thirty books. In 1962, *Traveling through the Dark* won the National Book Award for poetry.

Beverly Cleary was born in McMinnville in 1916. The creator of Ramona Quimby grew up in Portland. Her first book, *Henry Huggins,* was published in 1950. Cleary writes funny stories about children and their lives. In 1984, Cleary won the Newbery Award. It was for *Dear Mr. Henshaw.*

Ursula K. Le Guin was born in California in 1929. Later, she moved to Portland. Le Guin became a fantasy and science-fiction writer. In 1973, she won the National Book Award. It was for a chil-

Ernest Haycox wrote more than twenty novels and more than three hundred short stories.

Phyllis McGinley

dren's book, *The Furthest Shore*. Another book is *Searoad: Chronicles of Klatsland*. Its stories are set in coastal Oregon.

Ken Kesey was born in Colorado in 1935. He grew up in Springfield, Oregon. His best-known novel is *One Flew Over the Cuckoo's Nest. Sometimes a Great Notion* is set in an Oregon logging town.

Raymond Carver (1938-1988) was born in Clatskanie. He became a poet and short-story writer. By age nineteen, Raymond was a married father of two. For a time, he worked as a tulip-picker and janitor. Later, he wrote stories about working people in Oregon and Washington. *Will You Please Be Quiet, Please?* is a book of his stories.

Norton Simon (1907-1993) was born in Portland. Simon started running Hunt Foods in 1942. Four years later, he bought the Ohio Match Company. Later, he controlled *McCall's* magazine and Canada Dry. He began a fine art collection, too. Most of it is in California's Norton Simon Museum of Art.

Mel Blanc (1908-1989) was born in California. He grew up in Portland. He was known as the "Man with a Thousand Voices." Blanc became the voice for many cartoon characters. They included Bugs Bunny, Daffy Duck, and Barney Rubble.

Raymond Carver

Philip Knight was born in Portland in 1938. He became a star runner at the University of Oregon. His coach was **Bill Bowerman**. Bowerman was born in 1911 in eastern Oregon. He designed track shoes for his runners. In 1971, Knight and Bowerman founded Nike. A year later, Bowerman designed a new shoe sole. He poured rubber on his wife's waffle iron. Millions of runners have bought Nike shoes with waffle soles.

Many other great athletes were born in Portland. **Mickey Lolich** was born in 1940. At age eighteen, he signed with the Detroit Tigers. He became a star pitcher. Lolich pitched three winning games in the 1968 World Series. That made the Tigers world champions. **Dale Murphy** was born in 1956. He became a great home-run hitter. Murphy played for the Atlanta Braves. He won the 1984 and 1985 National League home-run titles. **Dick Fosbury** was born in 1947. He became a great high jumper. Fosbury flopped backward over the bar. It was called the Fosbury Flop. This changed the sport. Fosbury won the 1968 Olympic gold medal. He cleared the bar at 7 feet 4.25 inches. Fosbury entered the Track and Field Hall of Fame in 1981. **Ahmad Rashad** was born in 1949. He has had two careers. Rashad became a great pass receiver with

Mel Blanc

Mary Decker Slaney (on the right)

the Minnesota Vikings. He is now a television sportscaster.

Mary Decker Slaney was born in New Jersey in 1958. She became a runner. Slaney moved to Eugene to train. She holds five running records for American women. One of them is the fastest time for running the mile.

Howard Hesseman was born in Lebanon, Oregon in 1940. He became an actor. Hesseman played disk jockey Johnny Fever in "WKRP in Cincinnati" (1978-1982). He was also teacher Charlie Moore in "Head of the Class." **Sally Struthers** was born in Portland in 1947. She began acting right after high school. Struthers played Gloria in "All in the Family" (1971-1978). She won two Emmys for that role. Struthers was also the voice of teenaged Pebbles Flintstone. Today, she is a spokesperson for the Christian Children's Fund.

Matt Groening was born in Portland in 1954. As a boy, he passed his drawings around in class. For that, he was sent to the principal's office. Now, a Groening drawing is worth over $25,000. Groening created "The Simpsons." More than 21 million people watch that show every week. In 1990, "The Simpsons" won an Emmy. It was for the best animated series on television.

The birthplace of Linus Pauling, Matt Groening, Beverly Cleary, and Dale Murphy . . .

Home also to John McLoughlin, Mel Blanc, Ursula K. Le Guin, and Mary Decker Slaney . . .

The site of the country's deepest lake and deepest canyon . . .

The leading producer of timber, filberts, grass seed, nickel, and pumice . . .

This is the Beaver State—Oregon!

High jumper Dick Fosbury doing the Fosbury Flop

Did You Know?

The Appaloosa is a white horse with dark spots. It was first bred long ago by the Nez Percé Indians.

Oregon minted its own coins in Oregon City in 1849. The $5 and $10 gold pieces were known as "beaver money" because they were stamped with a picture of a beaver. Today, a $10 Oregon beaver coin is worth about $40,000.

Oregon's coast has many unusual rock formations. Elephant Rock, Face Rock, and Haystack Rock look like their names.

In 1913, Clara Munson of Warrenton became the first woman mayor of a city west of the Rocky Mountains.

Oregon has the tallest coast Douglas fir (329 feet tall) and the tallest Rocky Mountain Douglas fir (158 feet tall) in the country.

Two Oregon towns are named Brothers and Sisters. Sisters was named for nearby peaks called the Three Sisters.

Oregon State University's athletic teams are called the Beavers. The University of Oregon teams are called the Ducks.

Oregon's state flower is the Oregon grape. Its berries are used to make jelly. But the Oregon grape is not a grape.

Portland's Vacuum Cleaner Museum has vacuum cleaners dating back to the 1870s.

Oregon has mountains named Tom-Dick-Harry and Three-Fingered-Jack.

Milton Wright was one of the first teachers at Sublimity College, founded in the town of Sublimity in 1858. He later became the father of Wilbur and Orville Wright, inventors of the airplane.

In January 1944, the *United Victory* was launched from Portland. It was the first "Victory Ship." That kind of cargo vessel swiftly carried supplies overseas during World War II.

About fifty years ago, Bourne was Oregon's smallest town. Only one person lived there. The town started in the 1870s as a gold-mining camp.

Barbara Roberts, a former Oregon secretary of state, became Oregon's first woman governor in 1991.

Now and then, meteorites, rocklike objects from space, strike the earth. The largest meteorite in the United States was discovered in Oregon's Willamette Valley in 1902. The Willamette Meteorite weighs about 31,000 pounds.

OREGON INFORMATION

State flag

Oregon grape

Meadowlark

Area: 97,073 square miles (the tenth-largest state)

Greatest Distance North to South: 294 miles

Greatest Distance East to West: 401 miles

Borders: Washington to the north; Idaho to the east; Nevada and California to the south; the Pacific Ocean to the west

Highest Point: Mount Hood, 11,239 feet above sea level

Lowest Point: The Pacific Ocean coastline, sea level

Hottest Recorded Temperature: 119° F. (at Prineville, on July 28, 1898, and Pendleton, on August 10, 1898)

Coldest Recorded Temperature: -54° F. (at Ukiah, on February 9, 1933, and at Seneca, on February 10, 1993)

Statehood: The thirty-third state, on February 14, 1859

Origin of Name: At one time, the Columbia River was called *Ouragon* (French for hurricane), or Oregon

Capital: Salem

Counties: 36

United States Representatives: 5

State Representatives: 60

State Senators: 30

State Song: "Oregon, My Oregon," by Henry B. Murtagh (music) and J. A. Buchanan (words)

State Motto: *Alis Volat Propriis,* (Latin, meaning "She Flies with Her Own Wings")

Nicknames: "Beaver State," "Pacific Wonderland," "End of the Trail"

State Seal: Adopted in 1859 **State Flag:** Adopted in 1925

State Colors: Navy blue and gold **State Flower:** Oregon grape

State Bird: Western meadowlark **State Fish:** Chinook salmon

State Rock: Thunder egg   **State Gemstone:** Oregon sunstone

State Nut: Hazelnut (filbert) **State Tree:** Douglas fir

State Insect: Oregon swallowtail butterfly

Some Mountains: Cascade, Klamath, Coast, Blue, Wallowa

Some Rivers: Columbia, Willamette, Clackamas, Deschutes, John Day, Snake, Rogue

Some Lakes: Upper Klamath, Crater, Malheur, Harney, Abert, Summer, Wallowa

Wildlife: Whales, sea lions, harbor seals, salmon, trout, sturgeon, shrimp, clams, beavers, river otters, bighorn sheep, mountain goats, black bears, deer, foxes, elk, pronghorn antelope, porcupines, rattlesnakes, lizards, western meadowlarks, puffins, pelicans, cormorants, swans, geese, ducks, cranes, owls, eagles, great blue herons, many other kinds of birds

Farm Products: Filberts (hazelnuts), grass seed, peppermint, flowers, winter pears, plums, blackberries, boysenberries, potatoes, onions, raspberries, strawberries, cherries, green peas, snap beans, sweet corn, grapes, apples, barley, wheat, hay, oats, sugar beets, beef cattle, milk, sheep, horses, chicken, hogs

Manufactured Products: Lumber, wood and paper products, frozen fruits and vegetables, canned and baked goods, machinery, scientific instruments, computers, computer software, plastics, metals

Fishing Products: Salmon, shrimp, crabs, tuna, sole, cod, clams

Mining Products: Crushed stone, sand and gravel, pumice, nickel, clay, gold

Population: 2,842,321, twenty-ninth among the states (1990 U.S. Census Bureau figures)

Major Cities (1990 Census):

City	Population	City	Population
Portland	437,319	Medford	46,951
Eugene	112,669	Corvallis	44,757
Salem	107,786	Springfield	44,683
Gresham	68,235	Hillsboro	37,520
Beaverton	53,310	Lake Oswego	30,576

Douglas fir

Thunder egg

Hazelnut (filbert)

OREGON HISTORY

13,000 B.C.—The first people reach Oregon

A.D. 1500—Many Indians, including the Chinook, Klamath, Modoc, Bannock, Cayuse, and Nez Percé, are living in Oregon

1543—Bartolomé Ferrelo, exploring for Spain, sails along Oregon's coast

1579—Francis Drake, an English explorer, sails along Oregon's coast

1778—English explorer James Cook arrives at Yaquina Bay

1792—American explorer Robert Gray sails into the Columbia River, which he names for his ship

1805—The Lewis and Clark Expedition reaches Oregon's Pacific Coast and builds Fort Clatsop near what is now Astoria

1811—John Jacob Astor's Pacific Fur Company begins Astoria, Oregon's first permanent non-Indian settlement

1818—The United States and England agree that both countries can trade for furs and settle in Oregon

1824—John McLoughlin, the "Father of Oregon," begins running the fur trade west of the Rocky Mountains for the Hudson's Bay Company

1843—The first large group takes the Oregon Trail; settlers at Champoeg organize a government for the Americans in the Willamette Valley

1846—The United States and England sign a treaty that makes present-day Washington and Oregon part of the United States; the *Oregon Spectator,* Oregon's first newspaper, is printed at Oregon City

1848—Oregon becomes a United States territory

1850—The Oregon Donation Land Act offers free land to settlers

1851-56—The Rogue River War is fought between Indians and settlers

Okonogan, an Astor fur-trading post

1855—Salem becomes the permanent capital

1859—On February 14, Oregon becomes the thirty-third state

1861-65—About 2,000 Oregonians fight Indian wars in Oregon
during the Civil War

1877—The Nez Percé Indians are defeated after a heroic fight

1878—Paiute and Bannock Indians rise up against settlers and are
quickly defeated

1883—The Northern Pacific Railway reaches Portland

1907—Oregon's Jonathan Bourne is the first U.S. senator elected
by popular vote

1912—Oregon becomes the sixth state to allow women to vote

1913—Oregon becomes the first state to adopt an effective
minimum-wage law

1917-18—Over 44,000 Oregonians help win World War I

1929-39—The Great Depression hurts farming, banking, and
manufacturing throughout the country

1937—The Bonneville Dam is completed

1941-45—Oregon sends about 150,000 men and women to help
win World War II

1960—Maurine Neuberger is elected as Oregon's first woman
U.S. senator

1964—Parts of western Oregon are hit by damaging floods

1971—Oregon passes the first law by any state prohibiting the
use of nonreturnable beverage bottles

1977—The Portland Trail Blazers win the NBA championship

1990—Oregon's population is 2,842,321

1991—The Oregon Educational Act for the 21st Century is
begun to improve Oregon schools; Barbara Roberts takes
office as Oregon's first woman governor

1993—The 150th birthday of the Oregon Trail is celebrated

1994—Forest fires rage through southwestern Oregon

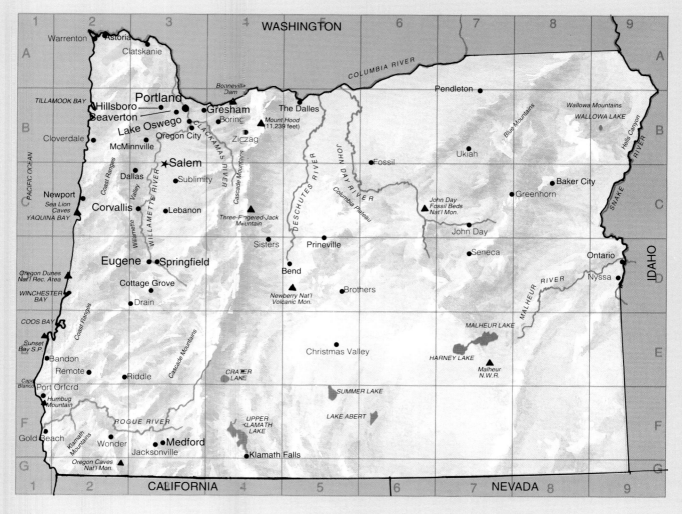

GLOSSARY

ancient: Relating to people or events of long ago

billion: A thousand million (1,000,000,000)

blowhole: A crack or hole in a rock through which ocean water spouts

canyon: A deep, steep-sided valley

capital: The city that is the seat of government

capitol: The building in which the government meets

century: A 100-year period

climate: The typical weather of a region

coast: The land along a large body of water

constitution: The framework for a country's government

desert: A large dry area of land

dune: A mound of sand piled up by the wind

environment: Surroundings such as air, water, and land

explorer: A person who visits and studies unknown lands

fossil: The remains of animals or plants that lived long ago

lava: Hot liquid rock from a volcano

million: A thousand thousand (1,000,000)

minority: A group of people who are different in some way from the largest group in the population

pioneer: A person who is among the first to move into a region

pollution: The harming or dirtying of the environment

population: The number of people in a place

pumice: A volcanic rock used for smoothing or polishing teeth or skin

replica: A copy, often life-size, of an original building, artwork, or other object

reservation (Indian): Land in the United States that has been set aside for American Indians

territory: Land owned by a country

volcano: A crack through which lava and other materials erupt; the mountain built by an eruption

Deep-sea fishing boats in Depoe Bay, said to be the world's smallest harbor

PICTURE ACKNOWLEDGMENTS

Front cover, ©Larry Geddis; 1, ©Larry Geddis; 2, Tom Dunnington; 3, ©Steve Terrill; 4-5, Tom Dunnington; 6-7, ©Larry Geddis; 8, ©Larry Geddis; 9 (top left), ©Jerry Hennen; 9 (top right), Courtesy of Hammond, Incorporated, Maplewood, New Jersey; 9 (bottom), ©Steve Terrill; 10, ©Terry Donnelly/Dembinsky Photo Assoc.; 11, ©Larry Geddis; 12, ©Greg Vaughn/Tom Stack & Assoc.; 13, ©Tom Till; 15, ©Buddy Mays/Travel Stock; 16 (left), ©J. Amos/H. Armstrong Roberts; 16 (right), ©Roger Bickel/N E Stock Photo; 17 (top), AP/Wide World Photos; 17 (bottom), Oregon Historical Society (OrHi248 #1707); 19, Oregon Historical Society (CN# 002665); 20, Oregon Historical Society (OrHi #4054); 21, Oregon Historical Society (Oreg.#4590); 22, ©Arnold J. Kaplan/Photri, Inc.; 23, AP/Wide World Photos; 25 (left), ©James Blank/Root Resources; 25 (right), ©Steve Terrill; 26, ©Steve Terrill; 27 (top), ©Steve Terrill; 27 (bottom), ©Joan Dunlop; 28 (top), ©David Falconer/Tony Stone Images, Inc.; 28 (bottom), ©Wayne Michael Lottinville/N E Stock Photo; 29, ©Steve Terrill; 30-31, ©Larry Geddis; 32, ©Buddy Mays/Travel Stock; 33, ©Steve Terrill; 34, ©Wayne Michael Lottinville/N E Stock Photo; 35 (both pictures), ©Larry Geddis; 36 (top), ©Greg Vaughn/Tom Stack & Associates; 36 (bottom), ©Larry Geddis; 37 (left), ©Larry Geddis; 37 (right), ©Wayne Michael Lottinville/N E Stock Photo; 38, ©Bob Pool/Tom Stack & Associates; 39 (both pictures), ©Wayne Michael Lottinville/N E Stock Photo; 40, ©Photri, Inc.; 41 (both pictures), ©Larry Ulrich/Tony Stone Images, Inc.; 42 (left), ©Ann & Myron Sutton/SuperStock; 42 (right), ©Roger Bickel/N E Stock Photo; 43, ©Roger Bickel/N E Stock Photo; 44, ©Larry Geddis; 45, ©Steve Terrill; 46, AP/Wide World Photos; 47, Oregon Historical Society (OrHi 49958 #072); 48 (both pictures), AP/Wide World Photos; 49, AP/Wide World Photos; 50, AP/Wide World Photos; 51, UPI/Bettmann; 52, UPI/Bettmann Newsphotos; 53, AP/Wide World Photos; 54 (top), ©Gemma Giannini; 54 (bottom), American Numismatic Assn.; 55, Oregon Historical Society/Donated by Mrs. Thomas H. Reynolds (OrHi# 56119); 56 (top), Courtesy Flag Research Center, Winchester, Massachusetts 01890; 56 (middle), ©Kitty Kohout/Root Resources; 56 (bottom), ©Rod Planck/Tony Stone Images, Inc.; 57 (top and bottom), ©Jerry Hennen; 57 (middle), ©Steve Terrill; 58, North Wind Picture Archives; 60, Tom Dunnington; 62, ©Larry Geddis; back cover, ©Larry Geddis

INDEX

Page numbers in boldface type indicate illustrations.

ABOUT THE AUTHORS

Dennis and Judith Fradin have coauthored several books in the From Sea to Shining Sea series. The Fradins both graduated from Northwestern University in 1967. Dennis has been a professional writer for twenty years, and has published 150 books. His works for Childrens Press include the Young People's Stories of Our States series, the Disaster! series, and the Thirteen Colonies series. Judith earned her M.A. in literature from Northwestern University and taught high-school and college English for many years. The Fradins, who are the parents of Anthony, Diana, and Michael, live in Evanston, Illinois.